Photograph by Ed Carpenter

ISBN- 978-1468096231
Printed in the United States of America

Joy K. Blair
P. O. Box 303
Florissant MO 63032

Joysready34@yahoo.com

Dedication

This Journal is dedicated to all the Entrepreneurs who desire God's guidance and complete control over their finances. God has a perfect plan for your finances and as you seek Him first daily, He will instruct you and teach you how to budget your checkbook, create wealth and invest in all the right places.

Salvation Prayer

If you have never accepted Jesus as your Lord and Savior, I would love to give you the opportunity to do so now. Repeat this prayer out loud: "God in Jesus name, I ask that you come into my heart. I believe that Jesus Christ is the Son of God and that He died on the cross for my sins and that He rose on the third day for me. Please forgive me for my sin according to Romans 10:9-10, in Jesus name, amen". If you have prayed this prayer, you are now born again. Please ask God to lead you to a local church home so that you can get the proper guidance and training. Read your Bible daily.

"The Lord My God Teaches Me to Profit"

(Isaiah 48:17)

Budget Planning Journal for Entrepreneur Women

Thus saith the LORD, thy Redeemer, the Holy One of Israel; I am the LORD thy God which teacheth thee to profit, which leadeth thee by the way that thou shouldest go. (Isaiah 48:17)

Date:_____

_____

_____

_____

_____

_____

_____

_____

_____

_____

_____

_____

Thus saith the LORD, thy Redeemer, the Holy One of Israel; I am the LORD thy God which teacheth thee to profit, which leadeth thee by the way that thou shouldest go. (Isaiah 48:17)

Date:_____

_____

_____

_____

_____

_____

_____

_____

_____

_____

_____

_____

_____

Thus saith the LORD, thy Redeemer, the Holy One of Israel; I am the LORD thy God which teacheth thee to profit, which leadeth thee by the way that thou shouldest go. (Isaiah 48:17)

Date:_____

_____

_____

_____

_____

_____

_____

_____

_____

_____

_____

_____

Thus saith the LORD, thy Redeemer, the Holy One of Israel; I am the LORD thy God which teacheth thee to profit, which leadeth thee by the way that thou shouldest go. (Isaiah 48:17)

Date:_____

_____

_____

_____

_____

_____

_____

_____

_____

_____

_____

_____

Thus saith the LORD, thy Redeemer, the Holy One of Israel; I am the LORD thy God which teacheth thee to profit, which leadeth thee by the way that thou shouldest go. (Isaiah 48:17)

Date:_____

_____

_____

_____

_____

_____

_____

_____

_____

_____

_____

_____

Thus saith the LORD, thy Redeemer, the Holy One of Israel; I am the LORD thy God which teacheth thee to profit, which leadeth thee by the way that thou shouldest go. (Isaiah 48:17)

Date:_____

_____

_____

_____

_____

_____

_____

_____

_____

_____

_____

_____

Thus saith the LORD, thy Redeemer, the Holy One of Israel; I am the LORD thy God which teacheth thee to profit, which leadeth thee by the way that thou shouldest go. (Isaiah 48:17)

Date:_____

_____

_____

_____

_____

_____

_____

_____

_____

_____

_____

_____

Thus saith the LORD, thy Redeemer, the Holy One of Israel; I am the LORD thy God which teacheth thee to profit, which leadeth thee by the way that thou shouldest go. (Isaiah 48:17)

Date:_____

_____

_____

_____

_____

_____

_____

_____

_____

_____

_____

_____

Thus saith the LORD, thy Redeemer, the Holy One of Israel; I am the LORD thy God which teacheth thee to profit, which leadeth thee by the way that thou shouldest go. (Isaiah 48:17)

Date:_____

_____

_____

_____

_____

_____

_____

_____

_____

_____

_____

Thus saith the LORD, thy Redeemer, the Holy One of Israel; I am the LORD thy God which teacheth thee to profit, which leadeth thee by the way that thou shouldest go. (Isaiah 48:17)

Date:_____

_____

_____

_____

_____

_____

_____

_____

_____

_____

_____

_____

Thus saith the LORD, thy Redeemer, the Holy One of Israel; I am the LORD thy God which teacheth thee to profit, which leadeth thee by the way that thou shouldest go. (Isaiah 48:17)

Date:_____

_____

_____

_____

_____

_____

_____

_____

_____

_____

_____

_____

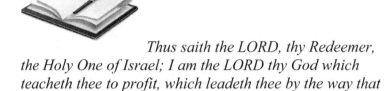

Thus saith the LORD, thy Redeemer, the Holy One of Israel; I am the LORD thy God which teacheth thee to profit, which leadeth thee by the way that thou shouldest go. (Isaiah 48:17)

Date:_____

_____

_____

_____

_____

_____

_____

_____

_____

_____

_____

_____

Thus saith the LORD, thy Redeemer, the Holy One of Israel; I am the LORD thy God which teacheth thee to profit, which leadeth thee by the way that thou shouldest go. (Isaiah 48:17)

Date:_____

_____

_____

_____

_____

_____

_____

_____

_____

_____

_____

_____

Thus saith the LORD, thy Redeemer, the Holy One of Israel; I am the LORD thy God which teacheth thee to profit, which leadeth thee by the way that thou shouldest go. (Isaiah 48:17)

Date:_____

_____

_____

_____

_____

_____

_____

_____

_____

_____

_____

_____

_____

Thus saith the LORD, thy Redeemer, the Holy One of Israel; I am the LORD thy God which teacheth thee to profit, which leadeth thee by the way that thou shouldest go. (Isaiah 48:17)

Date:_____

_____

_____

_____

_____

_____

_____

_____

_____

_____

_____

_____

Thus saith the LORD, thy Redeemer, the Holy One of Israel; I am the LORD thy God which teacheth thee to profit, which leadeth thee by the way that thou shouldest go. (Isaiah 48:17)

Date:_____

_____

_____

_____

_____

_____

_____

_____

_____

_____

_____

_____

_____

Thus saith the LORD, thy Redeemer, the Holy One of Israel; I am the LORD thy God which teacheth thee to profit, which leadeth thee by the way that thou shouldest go. (Isaiah 48:17)

Date:_____

_____

_____

_____

_____

_____

_____

_____

_____

_____

_____

_____

Thus saith the LORD, thy Redeemer, the Holy One of Israel; I am the LORD thy God which teacheth thee to profit, which leadeth thee by the way that thou shouldest go. (Isaiah 48:17)

Date:_____

_____

_____

_____

_____

_____

_____

_____

_____

_____

_____

_____

_____

_____

Thus saith the LORD, thy Redeemer, the Holy One of Israel; I am the LORD thy God which teacheth thee to profit, which leadeth thee by the way that thou shouldest go. (Isaiah 48:17)

Date:_____

_____

_____

_____

_____

_____

_____

_____

_____

_____

_____

_____

Thus saith the LORD, thy Redeemer, the Holy One of Israel; I am the LORD thy God which teacheth thee to profit, which leadeth thee by the way that thou shouldest go. (Isaiah 48:17)

Date:_____

_____

_____

_____

_____

_____

_____

_____

_____

_____

_____

_____

Thus saith the LORD, thy Redeemer, the Holy One of Israel; I am the LORD thy God which teacheth thee to profit, which leadeth thee by the way that thou shouldest go. (Isaiah 48:17)

Date:_____

_____

_____

_____

_____

_____

_____

_____

_____

_____

_____

_____

Thus saith the LORD, thy Redeemer, the Holy One of Israel; I am the LORD thy God which teacheth thee to profit, which leadeth thee by the way that thou shouldest go. (Isaiah 48:17)

Date:_____

_____

_____

_____

_____

_____

_____

_____

_____

_____

_____

_____

_____

Thus saith the LORD, thy Redeemer, the Holy One of Israel; I am the LORD thy God which teacheth thee to profit, which leadeth thee by the way that thou shouldest go. (Isaiah 48:17)

Date:_____

_____

_____

_____

_____

_____

_____

_____

_____

_____

_____

_____

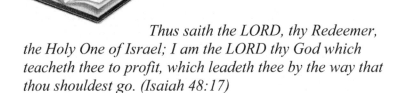

Thus saith the LORD, thy Redeemer, the Holy One of Israel; I am the LORD thy God which teacheth thee to profit, which leadeth thee by the way that thou shouldest go. (Isaiah 48:17)

Date:_____

_____

_____

_____

_____

_____

_____

_____

_____

_____

_____

_____

Thus saith the LORD, thy Redeemer, the Holy One of Israel; I am the LORD thy God which teacheth thee to profit, which leadeth thee by the way that thou shouldest go. (Isaiah 48:17)

Date:_____

_____

_____

_____

_____

_____

_____

_____

_____

_____

_____

_____

Thus saith the LORD, thy Redeemer, the Holy One of Israel; I am the LORD thy God which teacheth thee to profit, which leadeth thee by the way that thou shouldest go. (Isaiah 48:17)

Date:_____

_____

_____

_____

_____

_____

_____

_____

_____

_____

_____

_____

_____

Thus saith the LORD, thy Redeemer, the Holy One of Israel; I am the LORD thy God which teacheth thee to profit, which leadeth thee by the way that thou shouldest go. (Isaiah 48:17)

Date:_____

_____

_____

_____

_____

_____

_____

_____

_____

_____

_____

_____

Thus saith the LORD, thy Redeemer, the Holy One of Israel; I am the LORD thy God which teacheth thee to profit, which leadeth thee by the way that thou shouldest go. (Isaiah 48:17)

Date:_____

_____

_____

_____

_____

_____

_____

_____

_____

_____

_____

_____

Thus saith the LORD, thy Redeemer, the Holy One of Israel; I am the LORD thy God which teacheth thee to profit, which leadeth thee by the way that thou shouldest go. (Isaiah 48:17)

Date:_____

_____

_____

_____

_____

_____

_____

_____

_____

_____

_____

_____

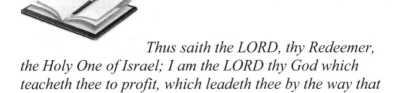

Thus saith the LORD, thy Redeemer, the Holy One of Israel; I am the LORD thy God which teacheth thee to profit, which leadeth thee by the way that thou shouldest go. (Isaiah 48:17)

Date:_____

_____

_____

_____

_____

_____

_____

_____

_____

_____

_____

_____

_____

Thus saith the LORD, thy Redeemer, the Holy One of Israel; I am the LORD thy God which teacheth thee to profit, which leadeth thee by the way that thou shouldest go. (Isaiah 48:17)

Date:_____

_____

_____

_____

_____

_____

_____

_____

_____

_____

_____

_____

_____

Thus saith the LORD, thy Redeemer, the Holy One of Israel; I am the LORD thy God which teacheth thee to profit, which leadeth thee by the way that thou shouldest go. (Isaiah 48:17)

Date:_____

_____

_____

_____

_____

_____

_____

_____

_____

_____

_____

_____

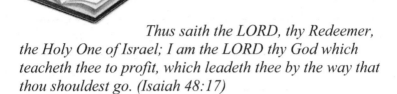

Thus saith the LORD, thy Redeemer, the Holy One of Israel; I am the LORD thy God which teacheth thee to profit, which leadeth thee by the way that thou shouldest go. (Isaiah 48:17)

Date:_____

_____

_____

_____

_____

_____

_____

_____

_____

_____

_____

_____

Thus saith the LORD, thy Redeemer, the Holy One of Israel; I am the LORD thy God which teacheth thee to profit, which leadeth thee by the way that thou shouldest go. (Isaiah 48:17)

Date:_____

_____

_____

_____

_____

_____

_____

_____

_____

_____

_____

_____

Thus saith the LORD, thy Redeemer, the Holy One of Israel; I am the LORD thy God which teacheth thee to profit, which leadeth thee by the way that thou shouldest go. (Isaiah 48:17)

Date:_____

_____

_____

_____

_____

_____

_____

_____

_____

_____

_____

_____

_____

_____

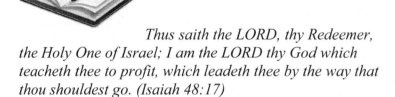

Thus saith the LORD, thy Redeemer, the Holy One of Israel; I am the LORD thy God which teacheth thee to profit, which leadeth thee by the way that thou shouldest go. (Isaiah 48:17)

Date:_____

_____

_____

_____

_____

_____

_____

_____

_____

_____

_____

_____

Thus saith the LORD, thy Redeemer, the Holy One of Israel; I am the LORD thy God which teacheth thee to profit, which leadeth thee by the way that thou shouldest go. (Isaiah 48:17)

Date:_____

_____

_____

_____

_____

_____

_____

_____

_____

_____

_____

_____

Thus saith the LORD, thy Redeemer, the Holy One of Israel; I am the LORD thy God which teacheth thee to profit, which leadeth thee by the way that thou shouldest go. (Isaiah 48:17)

Date:_____

_____

_____

_____

_____

_____

_____

_____

_____

_____

_____

_____

Thus saith the LORD, thy Redeemer, the Holy One of Israel; I am the LORD thy God which teacheth thee to profit, which leadeth thee by the way that thou shouldest go. (Isaiah 48:17)

Date:_____

_____

_____

_____

_____

_____

_____

_____

_____

_____

_____

_____

Thus saith the LORD, thy Redeemer, the Holy One of Israel; I am the LORD thy God which teacheth thee to profit, which leadeth thee by the way that thou shouldest go. (Isaiah 48:17)

Date:_____

_____

_____

_____

_____

_____

_____

_____

_____

_____

_____

_____

Thus saith the LORD, thy Redeemer, the Holy One of Israel; I am the LORD thy God which teacheth thee to profit, which leadeth thee by the way that thou shouldest go. (Isaiah 48:17)

Date:_____

_____

_____

_____

_____

_____

_____

_____

_____

_____

_____

_____

_____

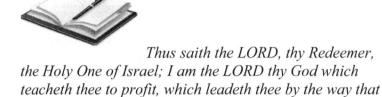

Thus saith the LORD, thy Redeemer, the Holy One of Israel; I am the LORD thy God which teacheth thee to profit, which leadeth thee by the way that thou shouldest go. (Isaiah 48:17)

Date:_____

_____

_____

_____

_____

_____

_____

_____

_____

_____

_____

Thus saith the LORD, thy Redeemer, the Holy One of Israel; I am the LORD thy God which teacheth thee to profit, which leadeth thee by the way that thou shouldest go. (Isaiah 48:17)

Date:_____

_____

_____

_____

_____

_____

_____

_____

_____

_____

_____

_____

Thus saith the LORD, thy Redeemer, the Holy One of Israel; I am the LORD thy God which teacheth thee to profit, which leadeth thee by the way that thou shouldest go. (Isaiah 48:17)

Date:_____

_____

_____

_____

_____

_____

_____

_____

_____

_____

_____

_____

Thus saith the LORD, thy Redeemer, the Holy One of Israel; I am the LORD thy God which teacheth thee to profit, which leadeth thee by the way that thou shouldest go. (Isaiah 48:17)

Date:_____

_____

_____

_____

_____

_____

_____

_____

_____

_____

_____

Thus saith the LORD, thy Redeemer, the Holy One of Israel; I am the LORD thy God which teacheth thee to profit, which leadeth thee by the way that thou shouldest go. (Isaiah 48:17)

Date:_____

_____

_____

_____

_____

_____

_____

_____

_____

_____

_____

Thus saith the LORD, thy Redeemer, the Holy One of Israel; I am the LORD thy God which teacheth thee to profit, which leadeth thee by the way that thou shouldest go. (Isaiah 48:17)

Date:_____

_____

_____

_____

_____

_____

_____

_____

_____

_____

_____

_____

Thus saith the LORD, thy Redeemer, the Holy One of Israel; I am the LORD thy God which teacheth thee to profit, which leadeth thee by the way that thou shouldest go. (Isaiah 48:17)

Date:_____

_____

_____

_____

_____

_____

_____

_____

_____

_____

_____

_____

_____

Thus saith the LORD, thy Redeemer, the Holy One of Israel; I am the LORD thy God which teacheth thee to profit, which leadeth thee by the way that thou shouldest go. (Isaiah 48:17)

Date:_____

_____

_____

_____

_____

_____

_____

_____

_____

_____

_____

_____

Thus saith the LORD, thy Redeemer, the Holy One of Israel; I am the LORD thy God which teacheth thee to profit, which leadeth thee by the way that thou shouldest go. (Isaiah 48:17)

Date:_____

_____

_____

_____

_____

_____

_____

_____

_____

_____

_____

_____

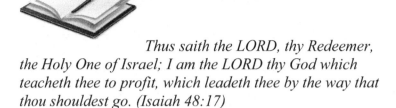

Thus saith the LORD, thy Redeemer, the Holy One of Israel; I am the LORD thy God which teacheth thee to profit, which leadeth thee by the way that thou shouldest go. (Isaiah 48:17)

Date:_____

_____

_____

_____

_____

_____

_____

_____

_____

_____

_____

_____

_____

Thus saith the LORD, thy Redeemer, the Holy One of Israel; I am the LORD thy God which teacheth thee to profit, which leadeth thee by the way that thou shouldest go. (Isaiah 48:17)

Date:_____

_____

_____

_____

_____

_____

_____

_____

_____

_____

_____

_____

Thus saith the LORD, thy Redeemer, the Holy One of Israel; I am the LORD thy God which teacheth thee to profit, which leadeth thee by the way that thou shouldest go. (Isaiah 48:17)

Date:_____

_____

_____

_____

_____

_____

_____

_____

_____

_____

_____

_____

Thus saith the LORD, thy Redeemer, the Holy One of Israel; I am the LORD thy God which teacheth thee to profit, which leadeth thee by the way that thou shouldest go. (Isaiah 48:17)

Date:_____

_____

_____

_____

_____

_____

_____

_____

_____

_____

_____

_____

_____

Thus saith the LORD, thy Redeemer, the Holy One of Israel; I am the LORD thy God which teacheth thee to profit, which leadeth thee by the way that thou shouldest go. (Isaiah 48:17)

Date:_____

_____

_____

_____

_____

_____

_____

_____

_____

_____

_____

_____

_____

Thus saith the LORD, thy Redeemer, the Holy One of Israel; I am the LORD thy God which teacheth thee to profit, which leadeth thee by the way that thou shouldest go. (Isaiah 48:17)

Date:_____

_____

_____

_____

_____

_____

_____

_____

_____

_____

_____

_____

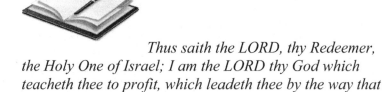

Thus saith the LORD, thy Redeemer, the Holy One of Israel; I am the LORD thy God which teacheth thee to profit, which leadeth thee by the way that thou shouldest go. (Isaiah 48:17)

Date:_____

_____

_____

_____

_____

_____

_____

_____

_____

_____

_____

_____

_____

Thus saith the LORD, thy Redeemer, the Holy One of Israel; I am the LORD thy God which teacheth thee to profit, which leadeth thee by the way that thou shouldest go. (Isaiah 48:17)

Date:_____

_____

_____

_____

_____

_____

_____

_____

_____

_____

_____

_____

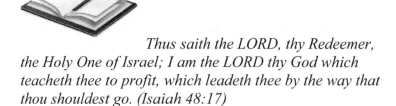

Thus saith the LORD, thy Redeemer, the Holy One of Israel; I am the LORD thy God which teacheth thee to profit, which leadeth thee by the way that thou shouldest go. (Isaiah 48:17)

Date:_____

_____

_____

_____

_____

_____

_____

_____

_____

_____

_____

_____

Thus saith the LORD, thy Redeemer, the Holy One of Israel; I am the LORD thy God which teacheth thee to profit, which leadeth thee by the way that thou shouldest go. (Isaiah 48:17)

Date:_____

_____

_____

_____

_____

_____

_____

_____

_____

_____

_____

_____

Thus saith the LORD, thy Redeemer, the Holy One of Israel; I am the LORD thy God which teacheth thee to profit, which leadeth thee by the way that thou shouldest go. (Isaiah 48:17)

Date:_____

_____

_____

_____

_____

_____

_____

_____

_____

_____

_____

_____

_____

Thus saith the LORD, thy Redeemer, the Holy One of Israel; I am the LORD thy God which teacheth thee to profit, which leadeth thee by the way that thou shouldest go. (Isaiah 48:17)

Date:_____

_____

_____

_____

_____

_____

_____

_____

_____

_____

_____

_____

_____

Thus saith the LORD, thy Redeemer, the Holy One of Israel; I am the LORD thy God which teacheth thee to profit, which leadeth thee by the way that thou shouldest go. (Isaiah 48:17)

Date:_____

_____

_____

_____

_____

_____

_____

_____

_____

_____

_____

_____

_____

Thus saith the LORD, thy Redeemer, the Holy One of Israel; I am the LORD thy God which teacheth thee to profit, which leadeth thee by the way that thou shouldest go. (Isaiah 48:17)

Date:_____

_____

_____

_____

_____

_____

_____

_____

_____

_____

_____

_____

Thus saith the LORD, thy Redeemer, the Holy One of Israel; I am the LORD thy God which teacheth thee to profit, which leadeth thee by the way that thou shouldest go. (Isaiah 48:17)

Date:_____

_____

_____

_____

_____

_____

_____

_____

_____

_____

_____

_____

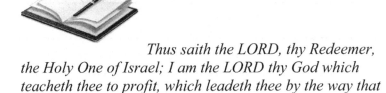

Thus saith the LORD, thy Redeemer, the Holy One of Israel; I am the LORD thy God which teacheth thee to profit, which leadeth thee by the way that thou shouldest go. (Isaiah 48:17)

Date:_____

_____

_____

_____

_____

_____

_____

_____

_____

_____

_____

_____

Thus saith the LORD, thy Redeemer, the Holy One of Israel; I am the LORD thy God which teacheth thee to profit, which leadeth thee by the way that thou shouldest go. (Isaiah 48:17)

Date:_____

_____

_____

_____

_____

_____

_____

_____

_____

_____

_____

_____

Thus saith the LORD, thy Redeemer, the Holy One of Israel; I am the LORD thy God which teacheth thee to profit, which leadeth thee by the way that thou shouldest go. (Isaiah 48:17)

Date:_____

_____

_____

_____

_____

_____

_____

_____

_____

_____

_____

_____

Thus saith the LORD, thy Redeemer, the Holy One of Israel; I am the LORD thy God which teacheth thee to profit, which leadeth thee by the way that thou shouldest go. (Isaiah 48:17)

Date:_____

_____

_____

_____

_____

_____

_____

_____

_____

_____

_____

Thus saith the LORD, thy Redeemer, the Holy One of Israel; I am the LORD thy God which teacheth thee to profit, which leadeth thee by the way that thou shouldest go. (Isaiah 48:17)

Date:_____

_____

_____

_____

_____

_____

_____

_____

_____

_____

_____

_____

Thus saith the LORD, thy Redeemer, the Holy One of Israel; I am the LORD thy God which teacheth thee to profit, which leadeth thee by the way that thou shouldest go. (Isaiah 48:17)

Date:_____

_____

_____

_____

_____

_____

_____

_____

_____

_____

_____

_____

Thus saith the LORD, thy Redeemer, the Holy One of Israel; I am the LORD thy God which teacheth thee to profit, which leadeth thee by the way that thou shouldest go. (Isaiah 48:17)

Date:_____

_____

_____

_____

_____

_____

_____

_____

_____

_____

_____

_____

Thus saith the LORD, thy Redeemer, the Holy One of Israel; I am the LORD thy God which teacheth thee to profit, which leadeth thee by the way that thou shouldest go. (Isaiah 48:17)

Date:_____

_____

_____

_____

_____

_____

_____

_____

_____

_____

_____

_____

_____

Thus saith the LORD, thy Redeemer, the Holy One of Israel; I am the LORD thy God which teacheth thee to profit, which leadeth thee by the way that thou shouldest go. (Isaiah 48:17)

Date:_____

_____

_____

_____

_____

_____

_____

_____

_____

_____

_____

_____

Thus saith the LORD, thy Redeemer, the Holy One of Israel; I am the LORD thy God which teacheth thee to profit, which leadeth thee by the way that thou shouldest go. (Isaiah 48:17)

Date:_____

_____

_____

_____

_____

_____

_____

_____

_____

_____

_____

_____

Thus saith the LORD, thy Redeemer, the Holy One of Israel; I am the LORD thy God which teacheth thee to profit, which leadeth thee by the way that thou shouldest go. (Isaiah 48:17)

Date:_____

_____

_____

_____

_____

_____

_____

_____

_____

_____

_____

_____

Thus saith the LORD, thy Redeemer, the Holy One of Israel; I am the LORD thy God which teacheth thee to profit, which leadeth thee by the way that thou shouldest go. (Isaiah 48:17)

Date:_____

_____

_____

_____

_____

_____

_____

_____

_____

_____

_____

_____

_____

Thus saith the LORD, thy Redeemer, the Holy One of Israel; I am the LORD thy God which teacheth thee to profit, which leadeth thee by the way that thou shouldest go. (Isaiah 48:17)

Date:_____

_____

_____

_____

_____

_____

_____

_____

_____

_____

_____

_____

_____

Thus saith the LORD, thy Redeemer, the Holy One of Israel; I am the LORD thy God which teacheth thee to profit, which leadeth thee by the way that thou shouldest go. (Isaiah 48:17)

Date:_____

_____

_____

_____

_____

_____

_____

_____

_____

_____

_____

_____

Thus saith the LORD, thy Redeemer, the Holy One of Israel; I am the LORD thy God which teacheth thee to profit, which leadeth thee by the way that thou shouldest go. (Isaiah 48:17)

Date:_____

_____

_____

_____

_____

_____

_____

_____

_____

_____

_____

_____

Thus saith the LORD, thy Redeemer, the Holy One of Israel; I am the LORD thy God which teacheth thee to profit, which leadeth thee by the way that thou shouldest go. (Isaiah 48:17)

Date:_____

_____

_____

_____

_____

_____

_____

_____

_____

_____

_____

_____

_____

Thus saith the LORD, thy Redeemer, the Holy One of Israel; I am the LORD thy God which teacheth thee to profit, which leadeth thee by the way that thou shouldest go. (Isaiah 48:17)

Date:_____

_____

_____

_____

_____

_____

_____

_____

_____

_____

_____

_____

Thus saith the LORD, thy Redeemer, the Holy One of Israel; I am the LORD thy God which teacheth thee to profit, which leadeth thee by the way that thou shouldest go. (Isaiah 48:17)

Date:_____

_____

_____

_____

_____

_____

_____

_____

_____

_____

_____

_____

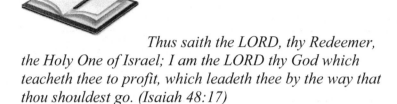

Thus saith the LORD, thy Redeemer, the Holy One of Israel; I am the LORD thy God which teacheth thee to profit, which leadeth thee by the way that thou shouldest go. (Isaiah 48:17)

Date:_____

_____

_____

_____

_____

_____

_____

_____

_____

_____

_____

_____

Thus saith the LORD, thy Redeemer, the Holy One of Israel; I am the LORD thy God which teacheth thee to profit, which leadeth thee by the way that thou shouldest go. (Isaiah 48:17)

Date:_____

_____

_____

_____

_____

_____

_____

_____

_____

_____

_____

_____

_____

Thus saith the LORD, thy Redeemer, the Holy One of Israel; I am the LORD thy God which teacheth thee to profit, which leadeth thee by the way that thou shouldest go. (Isaiah 48:17)

Date:_____

_____

_____

_____

_____

_____

_____

_____

_____

_____

_____

_____

Thus saith the LORD, thy Redeemer, the Holy One of Israel; I am the LORD thy God which teacheth thee to profit, which leadeth thee by the way that thou shouldest go. (Isaiah 48:17)

Date:_____

_____

_____

_____

_____

_____

_____

_____

_____

_____

_____

_____

Thus saith the LORD, thy Redeemer, the Holy One of Israel; I am the LORD thy God which teacheth thee to profit, which leadeth thee by the way that thou shouldest go. (Isaiah 48:17)

Date:_____

_____

_____

_____

_____

_____

_____

_____

_____

_____

_____

_____

Thus saith the LORD, thy Redeemer, the Holy One of Israel; I am the LORD thy God which teacheth thee to profit, which leadeth thee by the way that thou shouldest go. (Isaiah 48:17)

Date:_____

_____

_____

_____

_____

_____

_____

_____

_____

_____

_____

_____

Thus saith the LORD, thy Redeemer, the Holy One of Israel; I am the LORD thy God which teacheth thee to profit, which leadeth thee by the way that thou shouldest go. (Isaiah 48:17)

Date:_____

_____

_____

_____

_____

_____

_____

_____

_____

_____

_____

_____

Thus saith the LORD, thy Redeemer, the Holy One of Israel; I am the LORD thy God which teacheth thee to profit, which leadeth thee by the way that thou shouldest go. (Isaiah 48:17)

Date:_____

_____

_____

_____

_____

_____

_____

_____

_____

_____

_____

_____

_____

Thus saith the LORD, thy Redeemer, the Holy One of Israel; I am the LORD thy God which teacheth thee to profit, which leadeth thee by the way that thou shouldest go. (Isaiah 48:17)

Date:_____

_____

_____

_____

_____

_____

_____

_____

_____

_____

_____

_____

_____

Thus saith the LORD, thy Redeemer, the Holy One of Israel; I am the LORD thy God which teacheth thee to profit, which leadeth thee by the way that thou shouldest go. (Isaiah 48:17)

Date:_____

_____

_____

_____

_____

_____

_____

_____

_____

_____

_____

_____

Thus saith the LORD, thy Redeemer, the Holy One of Israel; I am the LORD thy God which teacheth thee to profit, which leadeth thee by the way that thou shouldest go. (Isaiah 48:17)

Date:_____

_____

_____

_____

_____

_____

_____

_____

_____

_____

_____

_____

Thus saith the LORD, thy Redeemer, the Holy One of Israel; I am the LORD thy God which teacheth thee to profit, which leadeth thee by the way that thou shouldest go. (Isaiah 48:17)

Date:_____

_____

_____

_____

_____

_____

_____

_____

_____

_____

_____

_____

_____

Thus saith the LORD, thy Redeemer, the Holy One of Israel; I am the LORD thy God which teacheth thee to profit, which leadeth thee by the way that thou shouldest go. (Isaiah 48:17)

Date:_____

_____

_____

_____

_____

_____

_____

_____

_____

_____

_____

_____

Thus saith the LORD, thy Redeemer, the Holy One of Israel; I am the LORD thy God which teacheth thee to profit, which leadeth thee by the way that thou shouldest go. (Isaiah 48:17)

Date:_____

_____

_____

_____

_____

_____

_____

_____

_____

_____

_____

_____

Thus saith the LORD, thy Redeemer, the Holy One of Israel; I am the LORD thy God which teacheth thee to profit, which leadeth thee by the way that thou shouldest go. (Isaiah 48:17)

Date:_____

_____

_____

_____

_____

_____

_____

_____

_____

_____

_____

_____

_____

Thus saith the LORD, thy Redeemer, the Holy One of Israel; I am the LORD thy God which teacheth thee to profit, which leadeth thee by the way that thou shouldest go. (Isaiah 48:17)

Date:_____

_____

_____

_____

_____

_____

_____

_____

_____

_____

_____

_____

_____

Thus saith the LORD, thy Redeemer, the Holy One of Israel; I am the LORD thy God which teacheth thee to profit, which leadeth thee by the way that thou shouldest go. (Isaiah 48:17)

Date:_____

_____

_____

_____

_____

_____

_____

_____

_____

_____

_____

_____

Thus saith the LORD, thy Redeemer, the Holy One of Israel; I am the LORD thy God which teacheth thee to profit, which leadeth thee by the way that thou shouldest go. (Isaiah 48:17)

Date:_____

_____

_____

_____

_____

_____

_____

_____

_____

_____

_____

_____